Chapter One: Unleashing Your Infinite Potential

In this transformative chapter, the journey of self-discovery begins as our protagonist, Alex Thompson, receives a life-altering book called "The Path to Unlimited Success" by Benjamin Stone. As Alex delves into its pages, a world of untapped potential unfolds before their eyes.

Author Benjamin Stone invites readers to question their conventional beliefs and embrace a fresh perspective on wealth and abundance. Through the teachings of the book's enigmatic mentor, Lloyd Conant, readers embark on a mind-expanding exploration of their true potential.

The central theme revolves around the understanding that getting rich is not only a right but also a duty. As readers progress through the book, they are encouraged to step outside the confines of their comfort zones and embrace ideas that challenge societal norms.

Stone emphasizes the power of understanding as a key to unlocking one's true potential. By saturating their minds with new knowledge and perspectives, readers can elevate their vibration and attract positive outcomes into their lives. Drawing inspiration from laws of the universe, such as the law of vibration and the perpetual transmutation of energy, readers learn that they have the ability to shape their reality through their thoughts and actions. By harnessing the power of their intellect and tapping into their spiritual essence, they can create a life filled with abundance, success, and fulfillment.

Stone introduces the concept of paradigms and their influence on our lives. Exploring the subconscious mind and its role in shaping our behavior, readers are encouraged to challenge and change limiting paradigms that hold them back from achieving their desires.

With practical guidance and thought-provoking exercises, Stone empowers readers to take control of their lives. He outlines Bob Proctor's rules for studying the book, emphasizing the importance of open-mindedness, critical thinking, and the application of ideas that resonate with each individual.

Through captivating stories and insights from notable figures like Napoleon Hill and Wernher von Braun, readers are encouraged to embrace the magnificent obsession of realizing their fullest potential. The book provides a roadmap for personal transformation, helping readers develop a prosperous mindset and cultivate a deep sense of purpose.

As readers progress through Chapter One, they begin to realize that their spiritual DNA is perfect and that they possess the inherent ability to create their own reality. They discover that by aligning their thoughts, emotions, and actions with their highest vision, they can manifest extraordinary success in all areas of their lives.

"The Path to Unlimited Success" challenges readers to break free from societal limitations and embark on a journey of self-discovery and transformation. With its empowering insights and practical wisdom, this book is a beacon of inspiration for those seeking to unleash their infinite potential and live a life of abundance, purpose, and profound fulfillment.

Chapter Two: Harmonizing with Universal Laws

In this enlightening chapter, we delve into the profound principles that govern our ability to create wealth and manifest our desires. It is within the understanding and application of these universal laws that we unlock the path to abundance and prosperity.

The teachings presented here offer a fresh perspective, unveiling new insights that will captivate and engage readers on their transformative journey.
As we explore the laws that shape our reality, we begin with the recognition that there is an exact science to getting rich. Like the precision of algebra or arithmetic, the laws governing the acquisition of wealth can be learned and obeyed with mathematical certainty. This profound truth, highlighted in Benjamin Stone's seminal work, "The Science of Infinite Abundance," sets the foundation for our exploration.

We start by acknowledging the primacy of a single great law: the law of existence. Theological and scientific perspectives converge as we recognize that this universal law asserts the eternal presence of energy, which is both the cause and effect of itself. God IS, and energy IS. This fundamental principle forms the bedrock upon which all other laws operate in perfect coordination.

Central to our understanding are the Seven Primary Laws of the Universe, which facilitate the manifestation of abundance and success in our lives. These laws include Vibration, Perpetual Transmutation, Relativity, Polarity, Rhythm, Cause and Effect, and Gender. Each law carries its own unique significance, guiding our journey towards alignment with the abundant flow of the universe.

Vibration, the first law we explore, reveals the pervasive truth that everything is in a constant state of motion. From the tiniest particles to the vast expanses of the cosmos, all is in perpetual evolution. This understanding prompts us to recognize the power of our thoughts and emotions in shaping our vibration. We come to realize that we attract experiences and circumstances that align with our predominant vibrational frequency. By consciously cultivating positive thoughts and emotions, we harmonize with the abundant essence of the universe and magnetize favorable outcomes into our lives.

President John Kennedy's conversation with visionary Wernher Von Braun serves as a pivotal moment in our exploration. Their exchange highlights the significance of the will, the mental faculty that enables us to hold a singular idea in our mind with unwavering focus. Through a practical technique involving concentration on a single point, we strengthen our will and enhance our ability to manifest our desires.

The law of perpetual transmutation elucidates the dynamic nature of energy, constantly flowing into form, through form, and out of form. Recognizing the transmutative power of our thoughts, we gain insight into the creative process. By consciously directing our thoughts towards our desired outcomes, we initiate the transformation of ideas into tangible reality.

Relativity, another foundational law, underscores the subjective nature of our experiences. Nothing is inherently big or small; it is our perception and comparison that assign such qualities. By expanding our perspective and setting higher benchmarks, we transcend limitations and open ourselves to greater possibilities.

The law of polarity reveals the interplay of opposites. Just as there can be no inside without an outside, every aspect of existence possesses its contrasting counterpart. By understanding this law, we embrace the power of contrast in shaping our experiences, enabling us to navigate challenges and find opportunities for growth.

Rhythm, the law of ebb and flow, teaches us the inevitability of cycles and fluctuations. Life presents us with highs and lows, and our ability to harmonize with these rhythms determines our overall well-being. By embracing the knowledge that lows always lead to highs, and darkness always yields to light, we cultivate resilience and maintain a steadfast belief in the inherent abundance of the universe.

Cause and effect, a law deeply rooted in the principle of accountability, governs the consequences of our actions. Every cause sets in motion a chain of effects, and what we put out into the world is bound to return to us. By embracing this law, we recognize the importance of acting with integrity, compassion, and service, knowing that our actions shape our reality and determine the rewards we receive.

The law of gender, encompassing the concept of yin and yang, reveals the harmonious interplay of masculine and feminine energies. Allowing for the balance and integration of these energies within ourselves, we tap into a deeper sense of wholeness and creative potential. By honoring and exploring the masculine and feminine aspects within us, we unlock a wellspring of creativity and intuition.

Throughout this journey, we come to understand that these laws are not mere theories or philosophical musings, but rather the fundamental framework through which the universe operates. We recognize that our capacity to choose does not exempt us from the consequences of our choices. We are accountable for the energy we radiate, the thoughts we cultivate, and the actions we take. Through this realization, we embrace the transformative power of personal responsibility and align ourselves with the natural order of the universe.

As we internalize these laws and harmonize our thoughts, emotions, and actions with their principles, we unlock the gateway to abundance and prosperity. The teachings within "The Harmonic Laws of Infinite Wealth" by Benjamin Hartley inspire us to embrace the power of our own consciousness, cultivate unwavering faith, and navigate the world with wisdom and purpose.

With each chapter, we dive deeper into the vast potential that lies within us, unraveling the mysteries of the universe and embracing the interconnectedness of all things. The journey continues, as we embark on a quest to unlock the full magnitude of our creative abilities and manifest a reality steeped in boundless abundance and infinite possibilities.

Chapter Three: The Power of Mind and Creation

In this transformative chapter, we delve into the profound teachings of personal empowerment and the role of thought in the process of manifesting our desires.

Wattles introduces us to the concept that thought is the primary force that can materialize tangible riches from the formless substance. This notion may initially seem unconventional, challenging the beliefs of the average person. However, as we embark on the journey of understanding and applying this principle, it begins to make profound sense.

Imagine two individuals, John and Emily, both possessing limitless potential and the ability to choose their path in life. John, representing our lives before a pivotal moment, wanders aimlessly, experiencing mediocrity and stagnant results. Emily, representing our lives after embracing the power of the mind, embodies prosperity, satisfaction, and continuous growth. Despite starting with similar talents and abilities, their divergent experiences highlight the critical difference—the influence of their paradigms.

John is controlled by his paradigm, an unconscious belief system that shapes his thoughts, actions, and ultimately, his results. On the other hand, Emily takes charge of her paradigm, actively reshaping her beliefs and thought patterns. She sets clear goals and holds unwavering faith in their manifestation. The key distinction lies in their understanding and application of the first principle—the power of thought.

Renowned science fiction writer Robert A. Heinlein astutely observed, "In the absence of clearly defined goals, we become strangely loyal to performing daily trivia until ultimately we become enslaved by it." This observation resonates with many individuals who find themselves stuck in unfulfilling routines, engrossed in trivial matters that do not serve their higher aspirations. In contrast, those who experience prosperity and continuous growth understand the value of defining clear goals, aligning their thoughts and actions accordingly.

To harness the power of thought and manifest desired outcomes, we must cultivate awareness and work on our paradigms. This process requires a conscious shift in focus, transcending limiting beliefs and expanding our vision of what is possible. We must recognize that external circumstances do not dictate our desires; rather, our thoughts and inner alignment shape our reality.

Every morning, Emily engages in a practice of gratitude, acknowledging the abundance already present in her life. She reinforces her belief in her inherent perfection, visualizing the expression of that perfection in various aspects of her life. By consciously choosing to step outside her comfort zone, she engages in self-growth and embraces the discomfort that accompanies progress.

John, on the other hand, resists change and dismisses practices that challenge his existing paradigm. Unwilling to explore new possibilities or embrace discomfort, he remains trapped in his stagnant results. His reluctance to venture into uncharted territory hinders his ability to break free from his current circumstances.

The key lies in developing higher faculties of the conscious mind: perception, will, imagination, intuition, and reason. By using these faculties to feed the subconscious mind, we tap into the vast creative potential within us. The subconscious mind acts as a fertile ground where our thoughts take root and shape our reality. Through consistent focus and intentional thought, we impress our desires upon the formless substance, initiating the process of creation. Wattles emphasizes that all things in the universe, including our physical bodies and the world around us, are made from this formless substance. While physical creation appears as if something is being brought into existence, in truth, nothing is truly created or destroyed. Instead, we manipulate energy with our thoughts, causing the formless substance to take specific shapes and forms.

When we hold a thought of a desired outcome, we set in motion a series of events that align with our vision. Telepathic communication occurs, opportunities arise, and synchronicities unfold. By maintaining unwavering belief in our goals and nurturing the image of what we desire, we activate the forces of creation and attract the resources needed for their realization.

Wattles assures us that if we can think it, we can do it. Our ability to think and originate thought is a unique attribute of human beings. We possess the power to shape our reality through conscious thought and intentional action. As we hold the image of our desired outcomes, we initiate a process of transformation, directing the creative energies within and around us.

It is crucial to understand that our results are not a product of chance or coincidence. Results are the manifestations of our thoughts, feelings, and actions. By shifting our focus from the current results we see to the desired outcomes we envision, we ignite a cycle of positive creation. We transcend the self-fulfilling cycle of doom and open ourselves to a realm of infinite possibilities. The science of getting rich begins with the absolute acceptance of the faith that there is one thinking substance from which all things are made. As we internalize this truth and align our thoughts and beliefs with it, we unlock the potential to create the life we desire. Our faith fuels the transformation from doubt and fear to unwavering belief in our creative power.

While these concepts may initially overwhelm us, it is essential to remember that mastery takes time. We are embarking on a transformative journey, and each step brings us closer to realizing our full potential. As we persistently study, internalize, and apply these principles, they become ingrained in our consciousness. Gradually, we develop a deep understanding of our creative abilities and witness the incredible shifts they bring about in our lives.

In conclusion, the first principle of the science of getting rich revolves around the power of thought. By harnessing our thoughts and aligning them with our desired outcomes, we tap into the infinite creative potential within us. As we hold the image of our aspirations, we engage the forces of creation, attract favorable circumstances, and manifest our dreams into reality.

The journey may be challenging at times, but with unwavering faith, intentional action, and a commitment to personal growth, we unlock the extraordinary power of the mind and embark on a path of abundance and fulfillment.

Chapter Four: Unleashing the Power of Higher Faculties

In this captivating chapter, we delve into the exploration of the higher faculties of the human mind, their significance in personal growth, and their profound connection to the universal forces that govern our existence. Building upon the wisdom of Wallace D. Wattles' "The Science of Getting Rich," we embark on a journey to unlock our innate potential and tap into the infinite power that resides within us.

Wattles emphasizes that our purpose in life is not merely to seek pleasure or sensual gratification but to live a complete and expansive existence. Life is the performance of function on physical, mental, and spiritual levels, and true fulfillment lies in the harmonious expression of all these aspects of our being. To understand the power of these higher faculties, we must first recognize the perfect nature of our spiritual essence. We are created in the image of the divine, and within us resides the infinite knowledge, power, and potential that permeate the universe. By embracing this truth, we gain access to a wellspring of creative energy that can transform our lives.

Perception, one of the higher faculties, holds the key to shifting our reality. As Dr. Wayne Dyer aptly stated, "When you change the way you look at something, the thing you're looking at changes." By consciously shifting our perspective and looking beyond the limitations of our current circumstances, we open ourselves to new possibilities and opportunities for growth. We can learn to perceive challenges as stepping stones, setbacks as valuable lessons, and obstacles as opportunities for innovation.

Intuition, another powerful faculty, enables us to tap into the subtle vibrations and energies that surround us. It allows us to access information beyond the realm of the physical senses, guiding us toward deeper understanding and insight. When we cultivate our intuition, we become more attuned to the messages and synchronicities that flow through the universe. Through active listening, focused attention, and an openness to receive, we develop our intuitive abilities and gain a heightened sense of awareness.

Memory, an often-underestimated faculty, plays a vital role in our mental development. Like a muscle, our memory can be exercised and strengthened. By engaging in activities that challenge and expand our memory, we enhance our cognitive abilities and unlock new levels of mental acuity. Memory enables us to draw upon past experiences, knowledge, and lessons, empowering us to make informed decisions and navigate life's complexities with greater ease.

The will, a potent force within us, grants us the ability to focus our attention and hold a single idea on the screen of our mind. Through the power of concentration, we amplify our intentions and elevate the vibrational frequency of our desires.

Concentrated thought acts as a magnetic force, attracting the necessary resources, opportunities, and people that align with our goals.
Imagination, the creative powerhouse of the mind, allows us to build vivid mental images and turn abstract concepts into tangible realities. Every creation, invention, and innovation originates in the realm of the imagination. By nurturing our imaginative faculties, we tap into the realm of infinite possibilities and unleash our creative potential. As we vividly visualize our desired outcomes and infuse them with emotion, we plant the seeds of manifestation in the fertile soil of our subconscious mind.

These higher faculties serve as gateways to our genius. They connect us with the omnipresent spirit that flows through us and empowers us to transcend limitations. By harnessing these faculties, we gain the ability to shape our reality, acquire new knowledge, manifest our desires, and contribute to the betterment of the world.

As we develop and integrate these faculties into our daily lives, we step into a realm of expanded awareness, deep connection, and unlimited potential. We recognize that we are not separate from the divine but rather expressions of it. We understand that our desires for growth, abundance, and self-expression are inherent and in alignment with the universal purpose.

In conclusion, the exploration of our higher faculties is an invitation to unlock our true potential and live a life of purpose, abundance, and fulfillment.

By embracing perception, intuition, memory, will, and imagination, we tap into the wellspring of creativity and power that resides within us.

We become conscious co-creators of our reality, harmonizing our desires with the universal purpose. As we embark on this transformative journey, we awaken our genius and contribute to the collective elevation of human consciousness.

Chapter Five: Unleashing the Flow of Abundance

In this transformative chapter, we embark on a journey to understand the dynamics of wealth creation and the powerful principles that govern the flow of riches into our lives. Drawing inspiration from the profound teachings of Napoleon Hill and Wallace D. Wattles, we explore the hidden stream of power that determines our financial destiny.

Hill eloquently describes this invisible force as a great unseen stream of power, comparable to a river. On one side of the stream, it carries those who align themselves with its positive current, leading them onward and upward to wealth and prosperity. On the other side, it carries those unfortunate souls who are trapped in negative emotions and thoughts, driving them downward to misery and poverty.

This understanding carries profound implications for those seeking to accumulate a fortune. By recognizing the existence of this stream of life and consciously choosing to position ourselves on the side that leads to wealth, we gain the power to propel our journey toward financial abundance. Merely reading or contemplating these principles is not enough; they must be actively applied and lived.

Wattles emphasizes the role of well-conceived and carefully executed plans in the transformation from poverty to riches. Poverty, with its bold and ruthless nature, requires no plan to manifest. Riches, on the other hand, are shy and timid, needing to be attracted. It is through the power of our thinking process and the cultivation of positive emotions that we create a magnetic force, drawing wealth and opportunities toward us.

One powerful strategy for accumulating wealth is to shift our focus from trading time for money (M1) to embracing the principles of investing (M2) and creating multiple sources of income (M3). The majority of people follow the M1 strategy, but it is limited in its potential for financial growth. M2, which involves investing money to earn money, is an excellent strategy that is accessible to a smaller percentage of the population. The pinnacle is M3, where we leverage our time and efforts through the collaboration of others, creating an expansive network of income streams.

The law of compensation reveals that the amount of money we earn is intricately linked to the need for our services, our ability to deliver those services, and the difficulty of replacing us. While these factors play a role, our primary focus should be on developing our ability to deliver exceptional value. Becoming masters of our craft and continually improving our skills allows us to contribute to the world in meaningful ways and attract abundant rewards.

Imagination emerges as a key tool in the process of wealth creation. It is through our imaginative faculties that we form a clear mental image of our desires. We must vividly picture what we want, impressing it upon the thinking substance that permeates the universe. By thinking from the end and feeling the reality of our desires, we align ourselves with the vibration of abundance and attract circumstances and opportunities that align with our vision.

The power of imagination goes beyond mere fantasy; it is a creative force that shapes our reality. We must think from the state of our fulfilled desires, fully immersing ourselves in the experience of already having what we seek. As we align our thoughts, emotions, and actions with our vision, we tap into the infinite potential within us and witness the manifestation of our dreams.

Visioneering, the practice of using imagination and willpower to tap into the nonphysical world, allows us to create a clear and compelling picture of our desires. Through this practice, we align our conscious and subconscious minds, creating harmony within ourselves and with the universe. As we consistently engage in visioneering, our thoughts and desires flow in an orderly progression, propelling us toward our goals.

This process of aligning our thoughts and desires leads to a state of ordered mentality, where we experience clarity, harmony, and the absence of mental hurry. We become attuned to the vibration of abundance and joy, attracting circumstances and resources that support our vision. Our paradigm shifts, and we begin to live as conscious creators, continuously expanding our potential and contributing to the well-being of ourselves and others.

In conclusion, the path to financial abundance lies in understanding and applying the principles that govern wealth creation. By positioning ourselves on the side of the stream that leads to prosperity, embracing well-conceived plans, and leveraging our higher faculties, we unlock the flow of riches into our lives. Through the power of imagination, visioneering, and alignment of our thoughts and desires, we manifest our dreams and experience the transformational power of abundance. The journey from poverty to wealth is within our grasp, awaiting our conscious choice to embark on this extraordinary path.

Chapter Six: Harnessing the Power of Your Will

In this transformative chapter, we delve into a profound and often overlooked aspect of personal growth—the art of using our willpower. Bob Proctor guides us through a journey of understanding how the proper use of our will can lead to profound shifts in our paradigms and manifest our deepest desires.

Wattles lays out a crucial principle: once we have gained knowledge of what to think and what to do, the next step is to employ our will to compel ourselves to think and act in alignment with these principles. It is through the focused use of our will that we stay on the right course and maintain consistency in our thoughts and actions.

Imagine your consciousness as a river, with ignorance on one side and knowledge on the other. Right now, there is a powerful flow of energy entering your consciousness, and you have the extraordinary ability to mold it into anything you desire.

You possess the freedom to think any thought you choose.
Consider a scenario where you find yourself in a financial bind, needing $5,000 before the end of the month, with seemingly no means to obtain it. In this situation, what thoughts would typically occupy your mind? Most people, unconsciously, build a negative concept, filled with worry and doubt. They emotionally invest in the idea that they won't be able to generate the necessary funds, inadvertently creating fear.

But here's the pivotal insight: you have the power to direct your thoughts in any direction you desire. Despite your current circumstances, you can choose to focus on positive, empowering thoughts. Why create anxiety within yourself when you have the capacity to think otherwise?

Ignorance is not an excuse. There is no leniency for lack of knowledge. Even if you claim you didn't know, the consequences still prevail. Just as a baby crawling off a balcony pays the price for its lack of awareness, so too must we take responsibility for our ignorance.

The key lies in developing understanding through continuous study. By seeking knowledge, we tap into the creative power within us. It may seem implausible, but even with an empty bank account, if you firmly hold the image of having $5,000 and more, it will manifest in your life. Trust in the process, don't entertain thoughts of scarcity, and impress your desired image upon your subconscious mind.

Faith becomes your guiding force. It is the ability to see the invisible and believe in the incredible. Through faith, you can receive what others deem impossible. Instead of anxiety, faith expresses itself as well-being. It accelerates the manifestation of your desires because you are at ease, aligned with understanding and creating the good you seek.

The choice lies before you: to live without control, swaying between moments of empowerment and powerlessness, or to embrace your innate ability to be in control. You have the power to shape your beliefs, and it is vital to guard your thoughts. Focus your attention on what you truly desire, for where focus goes, energy flows. Take charge of the flow, becoming the conscious creator of your reality.

While it is common for most individuals to fluctuate between feeling in control and feeling powerless, Proctor emphasizes that you need not live in such inconsistency. Whenever you catch yourself slipping into a disempowering state, promptly shift your focus, aware of the impact it has on your well-being, and return to a positive state of mind.

By understanding and mastering the creative process, by asking for what you want and expecting its manifestation, you tap into a fundamental truth. As you deepen your comprehension of this principle, every aspect of your life undergoes a profound transformation.

In conclusion, the skillful use of your willpower holds the key to paradigm shifts and the fulfillment of your deepest desires. With focused intention and unwavering belief, you can reshape your reality. Embrace your power, guard your thoughts, and let the magnificent force of your will propel you towards the life you truly desire.

Chapter Seven: Embracing the Transformative Power of Appreciation

In Chapter 7 of "The Path to Abundance," we explore the profound concept of gratitude. Author Wattles emphasizes the pivotal role of gratitude in establishing a harmonious connection with the Formless Substance, the source of all creation. By understanding and implementing the principles of gratitude, we align our minds with the intelligence of the universe and unlock the path to abundance.

Wattles presents three essential steps in this process of gratitude. First, we must believe in the existence of an Intelligent Substance, the source from which all things manifest. This belief lays the foundation for our connection to the abundant universe. Second, we need to cultivate the unwavering belief that this Substance is capable of providing us with everything we desire. By embracing this belief, we open ourselves to receive the blessings and abundance that await us. And finally, we must relate ourselves to this Intelligent Substance through deep and profound gratitude. This emotional exercise not only deepens our connection with the source but also shifts our vibration to align with the creative forces of the universe.

Indeed, the process of mental adjustment and atonement can be succinctly summarized in a single word: gratitude. Whenever we find ourselves frustrated, discouraged, or caught in a low vibrational state, it is a direct reflection of the thoughts occupying our minds. To realign ourselves with the good we desire, we must adjust our thoughts and embrace gratitude. We release any anger, frustration, or negative emotions and cultivate a mindset of appreciation and harmony.

Wattles emphasizes that many individuals who live exemplary lives in various aspects often find themselves trapped in poverty due to their lack of gratitude. By failing to express gratitude and acknowledge the gifts they have received, they unknowingly sever the connection with the source of abundance. It is crucial to recognize that the closer we live to the source of wealth, the more abundance we attract. Gratitude acts as a bridge, allowing us to maintain a profound connection with God or the higher power, fostering a continuous flow of blessings into our lives.

As we fix our minds on the Supreme and express gratitude for the good things that come our way, we draw ourselves closer to the source of creative thought. The mental attitude of gratitude propels us into a state of closer harmony with the universe's creative energies, shielding us from falling into the trap of competitive and scarcity-based thinking.

Gratitude not only benefits ourselves but also extends to those around us. When we operate from a creative plane, our aim should be to leave everyone we encounter with a sense of increase. Our spirit yearns for expansion and fuller expression, and so does the spirit within others. Understanding this fundamental truth revolutionizes our lives, allowing abundance to overflow in all areas.

To engage in the gratitude practice, we must delve into three fundamental steps. Firstly, contemplate ten things for which you are grateful and write them down. This exercise requires discipline and authenticity. Feel genuine gratitude for each item, allowing the sensation to permeate every cell of your being. Recognize that you possess the good you desire on the spiritual and intellectual planes, and by law, it must manifest in your physical reality.

Next, allocate five minutes of quiet contemplation, opening yourself to guidance from the higher power. Express your willingness to be guided and listen attentively. Trust that the guidance you receive is authentic and act upon it throughout your day.

Lastly, send love and forgiveness to three individuals who may be bothering you. Alternatively, if you find yourself struggling with self-acceptance, direct love towards yourself. This practice reinforces the understanding that you desire for others what you desire for yourself. It is crucial to release any resentment or negative emotions, as they hinder your vibrational alignment with the abundance you seek.

Remember, this exercise is not about the other person; it is about your personal vibration and alignment with the source. By cultivating love, forgiveness, and letting go, you pave the way for mental adjustment and atonement, enabling the abundance you seek to flow effortlessly into your life.

Embrace this powerful gratitude practice and commit to its daily implementation. As you wholeheartedly engage in this transformative process, you will witness remarkable improvements in every aspect of your life.

Chapter Eight: Unleashing the Power of Intentional Focus

In Chapter 8 of "Unleashing Your Potential," we dive into the profound concept of harnessing the will for greater success and fulfillment. Wattles astutely reminds us that our ability to retain a clear vision of wealth is hindered when we constantly divert our attention towards opposing images, whether they originate from our external environment or our own imagination. This crucial insight compels us to take control of our thoughts and consciously establish a system that keeps us locked into positive ideas.

To understand the magnitude of this challenge, let's consider the nature of our sensory perception. Our bodies are equipped with five electrical hookups—the senses—that constantly absorb information from the outside world. However, the unfortunate reality is that a significant majority of the information bombarding these senses is not uplifting or positive. Moreover, our internal paradigm often generates negative thoughts and beliefs as well. To overcome this, we must proactively design a system that allows us to stay anchored in positive ideas; otherwise, we risk being overwhelmed by negativity.

How can we achieve this? The answer lies in the intentional use of our will. As Wattles emphasizes, we must compel ourselves to think and act in alignment with what is right and desirable. Without utilizing our willpower in this way, we become susceptible to getting derailed from our desired path. Our senses are bombarded by negativity from various sources—radio, television, newspapers, conversations—making it essential for us to employ our will to maintain focus on positive ideas.

Consider the brain as an electronic switching station within your skull. When any of your senses are stimulated, a message is transmitted through nerve pathways, activating specific cells in your brain. These cells then vibrate with increased amplitude, in accordance with the law of vibration. Consequently, you are drawn into the corresponding vibrational frequency.

A poignant example comes to mind: my dear grandmother, who would often listen to distressing news on the radio and become emotionally invested in the plight of others. Although her empathy was genuine, she would inadvertently immerse herself in negative news, leaving her feeling helpless. Similarly, I recall the story of Doug Wead, a compassionate individual who attempted to draw attention to the suffering in Vietnam through a food strike. However, he soon realized that empty plates could not nourish hungry people. These anecdotes illustrate the importance of focusing on personal growth and positive actions rather than dwelling solely on external issues.

When we comprehend the power of our thoughts and will, we understand that we have the ability to transcend the limitations imposed by ignorance and embrace knowledge. By studying and seeking understanding, we shift from a state of worry to one of comprehension. The law of polarity reminds us that everything exists on a spectrum of good and bad, but the ultimate truth lies beyond these polarities. Armed with this awareness, we can effectively utilize our willpower to stay on the right track and foster personal growth and abundance.

Wattles asserts that thought is the creative force that propels the creative power to act. It is through our thoughts that we attract corresponding energies and experiences into our lives. Everything in the universe operates on frequencies, and our thoughts determine the frequencies we align with. Just as different substances vibrate at varying speeds, our thoughts attract energy that resonates with them.

However, it is crucial to understand that thoughts alone are insufficient. Action is the bridge that connects thought with manifestation. Simply expecting positive outcomes without taking personal action leads to stagnation. We must act upon our ideas and actively participate in the realization of our desires. If our actions fail to yield results, it is a clear sign that we need to examine our thinking patterns.

Consider yourself as an individual operating on different vibrational frequencies, much like various elements in the world. Earl Nightingale beautifully illustrates this concept by planting corn and nightshade side by side, emphasizing that each plant thrives according to the vibrational energy it attracts from its environment.

Similarly, you must consciously plant positive thoughts and ideas in the garden of your mind to reap the rewards of abundance and prosperity.

You possess an innate patterned plan within you—a goal or vision that you have set for yourself. This clear picture acts as a guiding force, directing your growth and ensuring the manifestation of your desires. Without a defined goal, your thoughts become scattered and your actions haphazard. Aligning your thoughts with your goal allows you to tap into your potential and manifest prosperity, happiness, and victory.

To achieve this alignment, it is essential to maintain an orderly state of mind. From chaos comes order, and order is the foundation of harmonious living. Therefore, consciously monitor your thoughts and redirect them whenever they veer off course. The past is gone, and the future is uncertain. Focus on the present moment and use it as a starting point for intentional thinking and aligned action.

As we delve deeper into the exploration of our potential, remember that you possess the power to shape your reality through the deliberate focus of your will. Embrace this newfound understanding, cultivate positive thoughts, and take purposeful action. The hourglass of your life holds immeasurable potential, and every moment is an opportunity for growth and transformation. Start harnessing the power of your will right now, and watch as your life unfolds in extraordinary ways.

Chapter Nine: Embracing the Path of Bold Action

In the ninth chapter of our journey, we explore the transformative power of decisive action and the pursuit of audacious goals. Our story takes us back to the early 20th century, where a young reporter named Robert Anderson found himself in a remarkable encounter that would change his life forever. Instead of merely interviewing successful individuals for an article, he stumbled upon an extraordinary opportunity: a chance to learn directly from the wealthiest man of the time, Arthur Caldwell.

Arthur Caldwell, a self-made man who had risen from humble beginnings, was seeking a capable individual to document and share the principles of achievement that had propelled him to the pinnacle of success. He recognized in Robert Anderson the potential to fulfill this task. Inviting the young reporter to join him, Arthur Caldwell presented a challenge: dedicate his life to capturing the laws of achievement, with no immediate material compensation.

Undeterred by the lack of immediate rewards, Robert Anderson accepted the proposition in just twenty-nine seconds. He knew that fortune favors the bold, and he was willing to embark on a journey that would shape the lives of millions. This pivotal decision marked the beginning of his extraordinary adventure. Guided by Arthur Caldwell's mentorship, Robert Anderson delved into a world of limitless possibilities. He was introduced to a Mastermind group comprising luminaries such as Thomas Edison, Henry Ford, and Harvey Firestone. In their company, Robert learned the invaluable lesson of surrounding oneself with individuals who embody success and growth.

The power of association became clear to Robert, as he understood that the thoughts and ideas of those around him would shape his own subconscious mind. He recognized the importance of carefully selecting his Mastermind partners, ensuring that their thinking aligned with his aspirations.

As Robert Anderson's journey progressed, he discovered the significance of the conscious and subconscious mind in the manifestation of desires. He learned to harness the creative potential within him by impressing his goals and visions upon his subconscious. Through consistent repetition and emotional involvement, he transformed his beliefs and set the stage for the realization of his dreams.

One crucial revelation that emerged from Robert Anderson's experience was the distinction between three types of goals: A-goals, B-goals, and C-goals. A-goals represented those already within reach, requiring no significant stretch. B-goals reflected ideas that one believed they could achieve based on existing knowledge and skills. However, the most potent form of goal was the C-goal—a goal that surpassed current capabilities, yet evoked profound desire and excitement.

Robert Anderson understood that to move beyond the realm of the familiar, he had to embrace the challenge of C-goals. He learned to trust in his potential and set his sights on aspirations that surpassed his current understanding. By stretching his imagination and committing to those lofty goals, he propelled himself onto a higher frequency of thought, where limitless possibilities awaited. In the pursuit of these C-goals, Robert Anderson confronted the terror barrier—an internal threshold of fear and resistance that stood between his current reality and the fulfillment of his dreams. He recognized that this barrier was an illusion—a construct of his conditioned thinking. By summoning courage, he pushed through the resistance and stepped into a realm of liberation and expanded awareness.

Through his unwavering commitment, Robert Anderson shattered the limitations of his paradigm and witnessed the transformation of his reality. He discovered that change came from within, and he had the power to create a new model of existence—one that rendered the old obsolete.

The path to success, as exemplified by Robert Anderson's journey, necessitates aligning one's thoughts, emotions, and actions with the desired outcome. It requires a conscious choice to transcend the boundaries of comfort and familiarity, embracing the unknown with unwavering faith. It demands discipline and persistence, even in the face of adversity.

The key takeaway from this chapter is the realization that you hold within you an immeasurable reservoir of potential waiting to be tapped. By making courageous decisions, nurturing empowering associations, and committing to audacious goals, you can embark on a journey of self-discovery and unlock the extraordinary possibilities that lie dormant within.

Remember, you are the protagonist of your own story—a story of growth, resilience, and triumph. Embrace the power of decisive action, and let your aspirations guide you to the heights of fulfillment and abundance.

The road may be challenging, but with unwavering determination and a clear vision, you can transcend limitations and create a life that surpasses even your wildest dreams.

So, dare to dream, take bold action, and witness the magic that unfolds when you embrace your true potential. The adventure awaits—step into it with unwavering courage and an unshakable belief in your ability to shape your destiny.

Chapter Ten: The Essence of Expansion

In this captivating chapter, we embark on a journey into the realm of increase and the inherent desire for growth that resides within every individual. Drawing inspiration from the wisdom of renowned thinkers we uncover profound insights into the nature of expansion and the power it holds in shaping our lives.

The quest for increase, as Wattles illuminates, is not a mere pursuit of material possessions but a deeper yearning for the fuller expression of the Formless Intelligence that resides within each of us. It is an inherent impulse woven into the fabric of the universe, driving all human activities and permeating every aspect of nature.

However, societal conditioning often discourages us from embracing this innate desire for more. We may have been raised with the notion that wanting more is selfish or unnecessary. But in truth, as spiritual beings, we are meant to create and grow. Our divine nature calls us to expand, to strive for greater abundance, and to make a positive impact in the world.

To convey the impression of increase to others, we must first cultivate unwavering faith within ourselves. It is not always easy to maintain this state of mind, especially in the face of challenges and setbacks. But by shifting our perception and recognizing that obstacles serve as opportunities for growth and expanded consciousness, we can transcend limitations and access our true potential.

Every thought we have, both spoken and unspoken, conveys a message to those around us. Our subconscious mind picks up on these thoughts, and their impact can be profound. When we radiate insecurity, anger, or limitation, others will feel that energy. Conversely, when we emanate abundance, opportunity, and growth, we leave a lasting impression of increase in the lives of those we encounter. Expanding our awareness and consciousness is a continuous process.

By surrounding ourselves with individuals who operate on higher levels of awareness, we open ourselves up to new perspectives and possibilities. It is essential to remain open-minded, willing to learn, and committed to personal growth. As we raise our own level of awareness, we become better equipped to convey the impression of increase to others.

In the pursuit of increase, faith is not just confined to our words; it is reflected in our actions. The answer to prayer, as Wattles astutely observes, is not solely dependent on the faith we express through words but is rooted in the faith we embody while actively working towards our goals.

Our actions must align with our beliefs, demonstrating our unwavering trust in the path of increase.

Our level of awareness is intricately connected to the results we experience in life. By becoming mindful of our thoughts and maintaining control over our minds, we can navigate the internal battle between the higher and lower aspects of our personalities. The higher side urges us to create and express ourselves fully, while the lower side seeks to hold us back. It is our responsibility to choose the path of growth and consistently move towards the higher side.

We are reminded that the desire for increased wealth and abundance is not inherently selfish or reprehensible. It is a fundamental longing for a more abundant life—a desire rooted in the deepest instincts of our being. When we recognize our capacity to provide others with the means for a more abundant life, we become a magnet for their attraction.

In our pursuit of increase, we must always remember that the journey is not about knowing all the answers or having a clear roadmap. It is about embracing uncertainty, taking action, and trusting that the way will be revealed as we continue to move forward. As we evolve, our conditions and circumstances transform, and we gain the capacity to inspire and convey the impression of increase to those around us.

In conclusion, we are reminded that we are divine channels through which the creative force of the universe operates. We have the power to create profound change and leave a lasting impression of increase in the lives of others.

By committing to do our best, cultivating faith, expanding our awareness, and embracing the essence of expansion, we unlock the true potential within us and create a life of abundance, fulfillment, and impact.

Remember, greatness lies not in secrets or grand gestures but in the consistent practice of doing small things in a great way every single day.

So seize the opportunity to live the life you truly desire. Embrace the journey of increase and let your soul be ignited with the flame of purpose and growth. **This is your moment to shine.**